Oxford Read and Dis

T0347197

All About Islands

James Styring

Contents

Introduction	3
1 What Is an Island?	4
2 Volcanic Islands	8
3 Tropical Islands	12
4 Amazing Island Species	16
5 Remote Islands	20
6 Big Islands	24
7 Man-Made Islands	28
8 Protecting Our Islands	32
Activities	36
Projects	52
Glossary	54
About *Read and Discover*	56

OXFORD
UNIVERSITY PRESS

OXFORD
UNIVERSITY PRESS

Great Clarendon Street, Oxford OX2 6DP

Oxford University Press is a department of the University of Oxford. It furthers the University's objective of excellence in research, scholarship, and education by publishing worldwide in

Oxford New York

Auckland Cape Town Dar es Salaam Hong Kong Karachi Kuala Lumpur Madrid Melbourne Mexico City Nairobi New Delhi Shanghai Taipei Toronto

With offices in

Argentina Austria Brazil Chile Czech Republic France Greece Guatemala Hungary Italy Japan Poland Portugal Singapore South Korea Switzerland Thailand Turkey Ukraine Vietnam

OXFORD and OXFORD ENGLISH are registered trade marks of Oxford University Press in the UK and in certain other countries

© Oxford University Press 2011

ISBN: 978 0 19 464503 4

An Audio Pack containing this book and an Audio download is also available, ISBN 978 0 19 402214 9

This book is also available as an e-Book, ISBN 978 0 19 410896 6.

An accompanying Activity Book is also available, ISBN 978 0 19 464513 3

Printed in China

This book is printed on paper from certified and well-managed sources.

ACKNOWLEDGEMENTS

Cover: Alamy (Maldives/Tibor Bognar)

Illustrations by: Kelly Kennedy pp 17, 23, 33; Alan Rowe pp 40, 42; Mark Ruffle pp 4 (map), 36, 52; Jane Smith pp 5 (islands), 38.

The Publishers would also like to thank the following for their kind permission to reproduce photographs and other copyright material: 123RF p. 20 (Michael Rosenwirth); Alamy pp. 6 (Four Thousand Islands/Ian Trower), 10 (Travel Pix), 11 (A & J Visage), 13 (ArteSub/coral reef, Visual&Written SL/ box jellyfish), 14 (Danita Delimont/Vanuatu), 16 (Reinhard Dirscherl),19 (Danita Delimont/baobab trees), 21 (Robert Harding Picture Library), 27 (Gerry Pearce), 29 (agefotostock), 30 (City Image/Burj Al Arab); The Bridgeman Art Library p. 15 (Study of a Dodo (oil on canvas), Hart, F (19th Century) / Royal Albert Memorial Museum, Exeter, Devon, UK); Getty Images pp. 6 (AFP/ Stringer/volcano forming an island), 8 (Adastra/ The Image Bank), 9 (Arctic Images/Iconica), 26 (New Zealand/ Pawel Toczynski/The Image Bank, weta/Gprentice/iStock), 28 (Studio250/iStock), 29 (Intha floating island/Frans Lemmens/ Corbis Unreleased), 32 (Barcroft Meida), 33 (Obofili); Gordon Buchanan p. 17 (Woolly Rat); Naturepl.com pp. 14 (Adam White/crab), 17 (Rod Williams/tree kangaroo), 25 (Stephen Kazlowski/arctic fox); Oxford University Press pp. 3, 4, 12 (Chantal Ferraro/Moment), 18, 22, 23, 24, 25 (polar bear); Reuters p 31 (STR Old); Science Photo Library pp. 7 (Nicholas Smythe), 35 (Svalbard Seed Vault plan/The Lighthouse); Shutterstock pp 19 (ring-tailed lemur/Meunierd), 30 (Palm Jumeirah/Andrew Ring), 34 (TAW4), 35 (Svalbard Global Seed Vault entrance/Borkowska Trippin).

With thanks to Chris Oxlade for content checking.

The author would like to dedicate this book to Freddy Marlowe Dilger.

Introduction

An island can be very small, or it can be big, with mountains, lakes, roads, and cities. Some islands are hot, but others are covered with ice. Some islands have animals and plants that don't live anywhere else. Only about 10% of people live on islands.

Do you live on an island?
What islands do you know?
What is the biggest island?
Do you know any of these islands?

Manhattan

Honshu

Iceland

Hong Kong

Hawaii

Now read and discover more about islands around the world!

1 What Is an Island?

An island is a piece of land with water all around it. There are many different types of island.

Where Are Islands?

Less than 30% of Earth's surface is land – there are seven continents and thousands of islands. Some islands are in the middle of an ocean, and others are near the mainland. Many islands are so small that you can't see them on this map.

Baffin Island
Greenland
NORTH AMERICA
Hawaii
Caribbean Sea
Pacific Ocean
Hispaniola
Equator
Galapagos Islands
SOUTH AMERICA
Easter Island

How Do Islands Form?

Islands can form in a lot of different ways. Some islands formed a long time ago. About 20,000 years ago, Earth was very, very cold. Lots of water from the oceans froze into ice, and the sea level went down everywhere. Later, Earth became warmer and a lot of the ice melted, and the sea level went up. Places that were valleys and mountains 20,000 years ago became seas and islands.

Sometimes, land can move away from the mainland to form an island. It takes thousands of years for islands to form in this way.

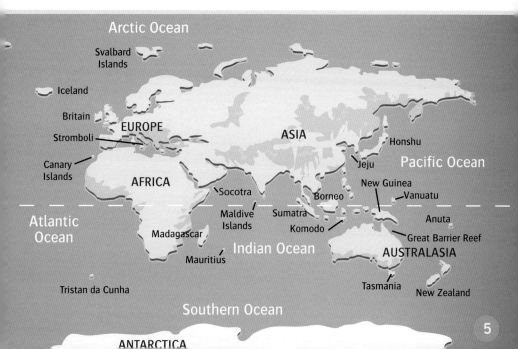

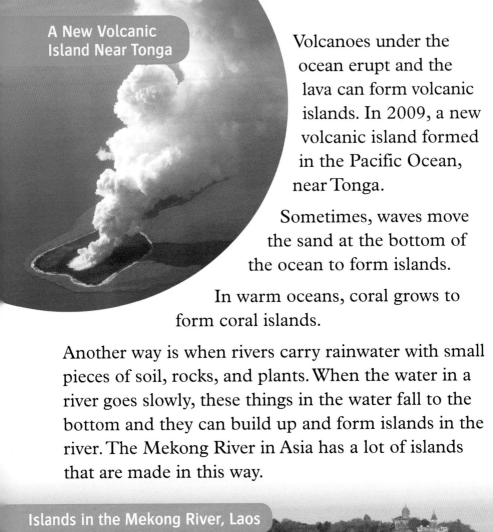

Volcanoes under the ocean erupt and the lava can form volcanic islands. In 2009, a new volcanic island formed in the Pacific Ocean, near Tonga.

Sometimes, waves move the sand at the bottom of the ocean to form islands.

In warm oceans, coral grows to form coral islands.

Another way is when rivers carry rainwater with small pieces of soil, rocks, and plants. When the water in a river goes slowly, these things in the water fall to the bottom and they can build up and form islands in the river. The Mekong River in Asia has a lot of islands that are made in this way.

Islands in the Mekong River, Laos

A Hispaniolan Solenodon

Amazing Species

The animals and plants on some islands grow in different ways from the species on the mainland. Some species live on only one island and nowhere else on Earth.

Hispaniolan solenodons live on one island called Hispaniola, in the Caribbean Sea. Solenodons are about 50 centimeters long. They have a long nose and they are the only mammal with poison in their teeth. They use their nose and teeth to hunt insects and other small animals.

Hispaniolan solenodons lived at the time of the dinosaurs, 65 million years ago! The solenodons are now in danger because people are cutting down the forests where they live, and dogs are hunting them, too. If we don't protect them, the last solenodons will die and the species will become extinct.

→ Go to pages 36–37 for activities.

Volcanic Islands

When volcanoes erupt, hot gases, ash, and lava fly into the air. When a volcano under the ocean erupts, the water cools the lava and it becomes rock. After lots of eruptions, the lava can form a volcanic island.

Active Volcanic Islands

There are thousands of volcanic islands, and some have active volcanoes. Mount Fuji on Honshu Island in Japan is an active volcano, but it hasn't erupted for more than 300 years. The volcano on Stromboli Island, in the Mediterranean Sea, erupts about every two hours! Some of the Canary Islands, in the Atlantic Ocean, have black beaches. This is because the lava from volcanoes forms a black rock when it cools. The wind and waves have changed the rock into sand.

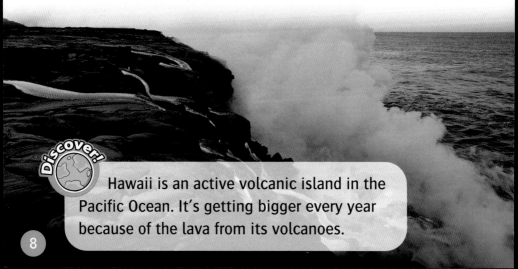

Discover! Hawaii is an active volcanic island in the Pacific Ocean. It's getting bigger every year because of the lava from its volcanoes.

Strokkur Geyser, Iceland

Hot Rock

The underground rock on volcanic islands is often very hot. When underground water meets hot volcanic rock, the water boils. Some of the hot water evaporates into steam, and the steam pushes the hot water up into the air. When this happens, the hot water is called a geyser. Iceland is a volcanic island with a lot of geysers. Iceland is cold, but even in winter, there are hot water pools where people can swim. Plants grow well in the warm ground near the geysers.

Discover!
Birds have to keep their eggs warm. Most birds sit on their eggs, but incubator birds on some volcanic islands leave their eggs in warm volcanic ash.

Plants on Volcanic Islands

After volcanoes erupt on islands, the lava cools and forms rock. Birds sometimes drop plants and seeds onto the rock when they are flying over. Plants can grow because the rock contains minerals. When the plants die, they form soil and then more plants grow. Plants grow very well in the fertile soil near extinct volcanoes on islands. After thousands of years, big forests can grow in fertile volcanic soil. Volcanic islands, like Borneo, Sumatra, New Guinea, and Jeju, have fertile soil and big forests.

Jeju Island, South Korea

A Rafflesia Arnoldii

Rice and tropical fruit grow well on volcanic islands in hot countries like Indonesia and the Philippines, and the forests are full of incredible plants. The world's biggest flower is the Rafflesia arnoldii – it can be 1 meter wide. It smells horrible! It grows in the forests on the island of Sumatra in Indonesia. There are very big trees on Sumatra, but every year people cut down more and more trees, and take the wood. This is a problem because one day, there will be no more big trees in the forests.

Discover!

There are about 17,500 islands in Indonesia, but people live on only about 6,000 of them.

Go to pages 38–39 for activities.

3 Tropical Islands

There are a lot of tropical islands near the equator in the Pacific Ocean, the Caribbean Sea, and the Indian Ocean. Tropical islands are warm and many of them are made of coral.

Coral Islands

Coral looks like a colorful plant, but it's a very small animal. Most corals live in warm, tropical seawater and when they die they produce hard skeletons. Corals grow in large groups, and millions of coral skeletons form underwater reefs. Waves push sand over a reef to form a coral island.

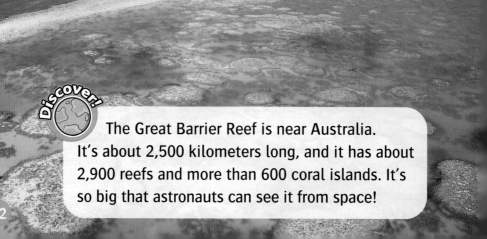

Discover! The Great Barrier Reef is near Australia. It's about 2,500 kilometers long, and it has about 2,900 reefs and more than 600 coral islands. It's so big that astronauts can see it from space!

starfish

A Coral Reef

Coral Reef Animals

More than 1,500 different species of fish and a lot of other animals live in coral reefs. Tropical fish are all the colors of the rainbow. Near coral reefs and islands, you can also find sea turtles and starfish.

Box jellyfish live around the Great Barrier Reef. They come from the same animal family as coral, but they look very different. Their legs are about 3 meters long, but they don't have much color, so they are hard to see. Box jellyfish are some of the most poisonous animals on Earth, and you should never touch them.

A Box Jellyfish

Pacific Islands

There are about 30,000 islands in the Pacific Ocean. The coconut crab lives on a lot of Pacific islands. It's one of the biggest land crabs on Earth and it's very strong. It can open a coconut with its legs!

A Coconut Crab

Bamboo plants grow tall and strong on many Pacific islands. People make houses from bamboo. Many people also eat young bamboo plants.

Discover!

On Pentecost Island in Vanuatu, the young men climb up bamboo towers that can be 35 meters tall. Then they dive toward the ground with ropes around their ankles!

A Painting of a Dodo

Mauritius

The dodo only lived on the island of Mauritius in the Indian Ocean. Birds usually fly away from danger, but thousands of years ago there weren't any other animals on Mauritius that hunted the dodo. The dodo didn't need to escape by flying, so it flew less and less every year. When Europeans came in 1507, the dodo wasn't scared and it couldn't fly. The Europeans' dogs, rats, and cats ate all the dodos. The last dodo died by about 1700, and the dodo became extinct.

Go to pages 40–41 for activities.

4 Amazing Island Species

Some islands have amazing species of animals and plants that don't live anywhere else. Most wild animals are scared of people, but some animals on islands aren't scared of anything. Do you know why?

Komodo Island

The Komodo dragon is the largest lizard on Earth. It's about 3 meters long. It has strong legs and a long tail. It only lives on Komodo Island and on three other small islands in Indonesia. The Komodo dragon can run and swim fast. It has sharp teeth and it has poison in its mouth. It eats deer and buffaloes – it even eats other Komodo dragons. Young Komodo dragons have to live in trees so that the adults can't eat them.

A Komodo Dragon

The Komodo dragon can smell things with its tongue!

A Tree Kangaroo

A Giant Woolly Rat

New Guinea

New Guinea is a big island in the Pacific Ocean, near Australia. The forests on this island are very wild, and there are places that people have never visited. Scientists keep discovering amazing, new species here. There's a kangaroo that lives in trees, and a giant woolly rat. The woolly rat is as big as a cat and it's the biggest rat on Earth! Most wild animals run away from people, but the woolly rat and the tree kangaroo aren't scared. This is because they have never seen people before, and they don't know that people hunt some animals.

Discover!

On New Guinea, scientists have also found a giant jumping spider and a frog with teeth like Dracula's!

Galapagos Tortoises

Galapagos Islands

The Galapagos Islands are in the Pacific Ocean, near Ecuador. The islands are famous for the Galapagos tortoise. There are important differences between the tortoises on the different Galapagos Islands. Some of the islands are dry, and some are rainy. The tortoises on the dry islands have a long neck. This helps them to eat the leaves of trees. The tortoises on the rainy islands have a short neck because they eat grass and other plants on the ground. These differences help scientists to understand how animals have grown differently in different places.

Madagascar Baobab Trees

Madagascar

There are about 10,000 species of plant on Madagascar, a big island in the Indian Ocean. Most of the plants don't live anywhere else. Madagascar baobab trees are huge – they can grow 30 meters tall and they can live for 1,000 years. Sometimes it doesn't rain for months, but the baobabs can live because they are full of water.

Discover!

There are about 60 types of lemur and they only live on Madagascar. A lemur uses its long tail to move in the trees, and to communicate with other lemurs.

Go to pages 42–43 for activities.

5 Remote Islands

It can be hard to live on islands that are very far from the mainland. On some remote islands, life hasn't changed for thousands of years.

Anuta

Anuta is a very remote island in the middle of the Pacific Ocean. About 250 people live on Anuta. They don't use money and they share everything. The weather is hot, so fruit like coconuts, papayas, and bananas grow well, but the island is tiny. Sometimes the people can't grow enough food, so they sail to another island where they have a garden!

Tristan da Cunha

Tristan da Cunha is one of the most remote islands on Earth. It's in the middle of the Atlantic Ocean. The weather isn't cold, but the Atlantic winds are strong. There are a lot of ocean birds, like albatrosses and penguins.

About 300 people live on Tristan da Cunha, and they share only eight family names. They are the families of the people who came to the island in 1816. They speak English. Most people are farmers or fishermen. There isn't an airport, and ships only visit a few times every year. In the past, it was hard to communicate with the rest of the world, but now people have telephones and the Internet.

Albatrosses on Tristan da Cunha

21

Easter Island

Easter Island is in the Pacific Ocean, 3,500 kilometers from Chile, in South America. Once, it had big forests and a lot of birds. Then more than 1,000 years ago, people came to the island in canoes. They built farms and towns, and for hundreds of years, they cut down a lot of forest trees to make houses, boats, and firewood. About 200 years ago, they cut down the last tree. Without wood, they couldn't make fires or build houses, and life was hard. A lot of the birds and animals died, and most of the people left Easter Island.

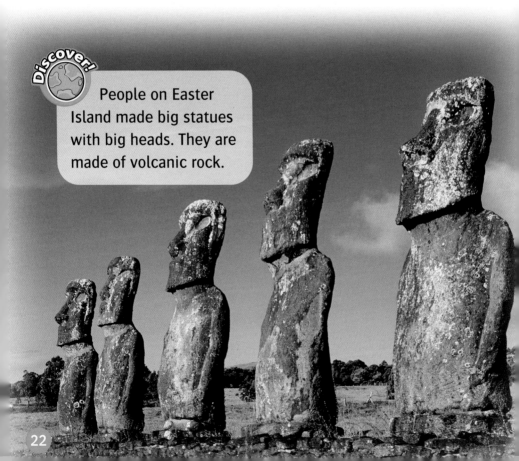

Discover!

People on Easter Island made big statues with big heads. They are made of volcanic rock.

Dragon's Blood Trees

Socotra

Socotra is an island in the Indian Ocean, near Somalia. It's very dry. Spiders and reptiles like snakes, lizards, and chameleons live there. Chameleons have hard skin and some can change color from green to pink, blue, red, orange, green, black, brown, or yellow! On Socotra there are 800 species of plant, and 30% of them don't live anywhere else. The Ancient Romans went to Socotra 2,000 years ago to collect the special red juice from inside the dragon's blood tree. They used the juice as a medicine.

Discover! A chameleon's eyes can look in two different places at the same time.

Go to pages 44–45 for activities.

Big Islands

Islands in the middle of the oceans are often small. The biggest islands are all near a continent. What big islands do you know?

The Biggest Islands

This picture of Earth shows the eight biggest islands. Greenland is the biggest island – it's more than 2 million square kilometers (km²). Some big islands, like Madagascar, are countries. Others are part of a bigger country, for example, Baffin Island is part of Canada. Some islands, like Honshu, have lots of people. Other islands, like New Guinea, don't have many people, but they have amazing plants and animals.

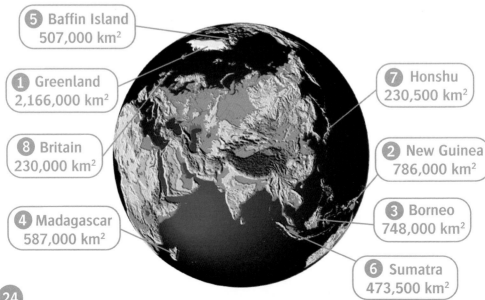

5 Baffin Island
507,000 km²

1 Greenland
2,166,000 km²

8 Britain
230,000 km²

4 Madagascar
587,000 km²

7 Honshu
230,500 km²

2 New Guinea
786,000 km²

3 Borneo
748,000 km²

6 Sumatra
473,500 km²

Greenland

Greenland is three times bigger than any other island. It isn't green – it's mostly white with ice and snow. There are almost no trees and only about 55,000 people live there. About 80% of the people are Inuit. Many Inuit people hunt and eat fish and seals.

A lot of the animals are white, like the Arctic fox, so other animals can't see them in the snow. The biggest animals here are the polar bears. They have huge paws so they can walk easily on the snow. They can run fast and they can swim more than 100 kilometers. In winter, they hunt seals. In summer, they don't eat very much.

Discover! Polar bears don't have white skin! Their white fur is about 5 centimeters thick, but they have black skin. Their black skin helps them to stay warm.

New Zealand

Most of New Zealand is two big islands called the North Island and the South Island. The islands are very different from each other. The South Island has a lot of big mountains – it even has some glaciers. The *Lord of the Rings* movies were filmed on the South Island. The North Island is volcanic, with geysers and hot water pools. People have lived on the islands for about 1,200 years.

A Weta

Three of New Zealand's birds can't fly. The most famous of these birds is the kiwi. The heaviest insect on Earth, the giant weta, also lives in New Zealand.

Tasmania

Tasmania is a big island about 240 kilometers south of the mainland of Australia.

The Tasmanian devil only lives on Tasmania. It's the same size as a small dog and when it's scared, it makes a horrible smell! The long hairs next to its nose help it to hunt for food at night. It has a strong mouth and sharp teeth for eating meat. It's noisy when it eats! Its favorite food is the wombat – an animal that only lives in Australasia.

Discover!

A Tasmanian devil that weighs 6 kilograms can eat 2 kilograms of meat at one time.

Go to pages 46–47 for activities.

Man-Made Islands

Some parts of the world are very busy and there isn't enough land for everyone. That's why people sometimes build new islands for farms, homes, stores, and airports.

Odaiba Island

City Islands

Sometimes people build cities on man-made islands. Odaiba Island is in Tokyo Bay in Japan. It was built about 150 years ago so that people could stop unfriendly ships coming to Tokyo. From about 1990, people built stores, restaurants, parks, and apartments on Odaiba Island. Today, Odaiba Island is a busy part of Tokyo City.

A Floating Island on Inle Lake

Floating Islands

The Intha people live by Inle Lake in Burma. Their houses are on wooden stilts that go into the water of the lake. They make floating islands with reeds, a type of thick grass. When the reeds are dry, they float on the water. On the islands, the Intha people grow rice and vegetables. They also go fishing in the lake for the fish that live under the islands.

Discover!

Intha men use their legs to row their boats.

Palm Jumeirah

Vacation Islands

In Dubai in the United Arab Emirates, tourists like the clear blue ocean, with pretty tropical fish and coral. The land is very dry and sandy, and there aren't enough beaches, so people have built islands in the ocean. The first area of man-made islands was Palm Jumeirah. It has hotels, stores, and thousands of homes.

Discover!

The Burj Al Arab in Dubai is one of the tallest hotels in the world – it's 321 meters tall. It looks like the sail of a boat and it's built on a small man-made island.

Airport Islands

Incheon International Airport in South Korea is built on a man-made island between two natural islands. Incheon is one of the busiest airports in the world, but it wasn't the first airport on a man-made island. Two Chinese airports and five Japanese airports are built on man-made islands, too. The first was Kansai International Airport in Japan.

Airports are often built on islands because there isn't enough land near big cities. Airport islands are big – about 4 kilometers long. They are often connected to the mainland by long bridges. The bridge from Incheon to the mainland is more than 20 kilometers long.

Incheon International Airport, South Korea

➔ Go to pages 48–49 for activities.

8 Protecting Our Islands

Earth's islands have amazing animals and plants, but life on islands is often in danger. Species can become extinct, and some islands could even disappear, so it's important to protect our islands.

Disappearing Islands

Our cars, factories, and power stations produce too many gases like carbon dioxide. Earth is getting warmer because there's too much carbon dioxide in the air. This is called global warming. Global warming means that there are more storms and rain. More ice is melting in the Arctic and the Antarctic, so the sea level is getting higher, and some islands are disappearing. A few islands between India and Bangladesh have already disappeared underwater.

An Island Disappearing

Some islands in the Pacific Ocean will probably disappear in 100 years – if we don't slow down global warming. Some of the Maldive Islands in the Indian Ocean will probably disappear sooner. Most of the land is less than 2 meters above sea level.

We can try to slow down global warming by making less carbon dioxide. We can drive and fly less, and we can use cleaner cars. We should use less coal and oil to make electricity. There are cleaner ways of making electricity.

Discover!

To help the Maldive Islands, people are designing new islands and towns that float! These islands won't disappear underwater.

Disappearing Species

Global warming is changing life on islands. When the sea level gets higher, some species don't have a place to live. Storms and floods can kill plants and animals. Coral dies when seawater gets too warm. Thousands of species live around coral reefs, but they can't live there if the coral is dead. We can help species on islands by slowing down global warming.

When too many tourists visit small islands, it's sometimes bad for plant and animal life. We can protect special islands by making them a conservation area. The islands in this photo are a conservation area in Thailand. They are a safe place for plants and animals to live.

Ang Thong Marine Park, Thailand

The Svalbard Global Seed Vault

Islands That Are Protecting Earth

The Svalbard Islands are in the Arctic Ocean.
Global warming probably won't melt Svalbard's
ice, and its high mountains probably won't disappear
underwater. This is why scientists from Norway
built the Svalbard Global Seed Vault there in 2008.
It's a place where they will store an example of each
of Earth's 1.5 million seeds. A plant could disappear
because of global warming or a natural disaster, but
it won't become extinct. That's because people can
grow another plant from the seeds in the Global
Seed Vault.

Discover! The Global Seed
Vault is inside a rocky
mountain at the end of
a long tunnel. Most seeds will stay fresh at minus
18 degrees centigrade for 20,000 years!

Go to pages 50–51 for activities.

1 What Is an Island?

← Read pages 4–7.

1 Write the words.

Europe Asia ~~North America~~ Africa
Australasia Antarctica South America

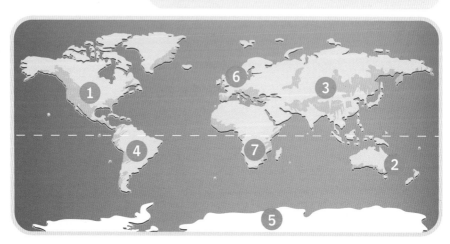

1 North America 2 _____ 3 _____

4 _____ 5 _____ 6 _____

7 _____

2 Write *true* or *false*.

1 More than 30% of Earth's surface is islands.   false

2 There are seven continents.   _____

3 Volcanoes can form new islands.   _____

4 Land can move away from the mainland
   to form an island.   _____

5 The sea level was higher 20,000 years ago.   _____

6 Hispaniola is in the Pacific Ocean.   _____

3 Match.

1 More than 70% of
2 Less than 30% of
3 Sometimes waves
4 Volcanoes under the ocean
5 Some valleys and mountains
6 Solenodons

move sand to form islands.
live on Hispaniola.
Earth's surface is water.
Earth's surface is land.
can form new islands.
became seas and islands.

4 Answer the questions.

1 What is an island?

An island is a piece of land with water all around it.

2 How many islands are there?

_____

3 Do you live on the mainland or on an island?

_____

5 Write about some islands that you know.

_____

_____

_____

_____

_____

_____

2 Volcanic Islands

← Read pages 8–11.

1 Is it an island? Write *yes* or *no*.

1 Mount Fuji   _no_   6 Strokkur   _____

2 Honshu   _____   7 Iceland   _____

3 Stromboli   _____   8 Sumatra   _____

4 Jeju   _____   9 Atlantic   _____

5 Hawaii   _____   10 Indonesia   _____

2 Write the numbers.

How a Geyser Works:

1 Water goes underground.

2 Water meets hot volcanic rocks.

3 The water boils.

4 Hot water goes up.

5 The hot water makes a geyser.

6 There are also hot water pools.

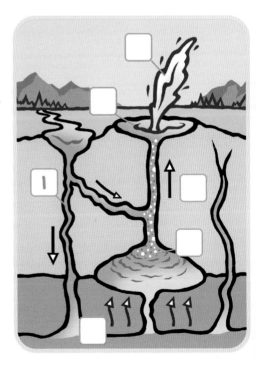

3 Complete the sentences.

   1 17,500   2 ~~300~~ 6,000

   1 Mount Fuji erupted more than __300__ years ago.

   2 The volcano on Stromboli Island erupts about every
      _____ hours.

   3 A Rafflesia arnoldii flower can be _____ meter wide.

   4 There are about _____ islands in Indonesia.

   5 People live on about _____ of Indonesia's islands.

4 Answer the questions.

   1 What forms a volcanic island?

      _____

   2 Which islands have black beaches?

      _____

   3 Where do incubator birds put their eggs?

      _____

   4 Why do plants grow well near extinct volcanoes?

      _____

   5 What grows well in the Philippines?

      _____

   6 Do you live near a volcano?

      _____

3 Tropical Islands

← Read pages 12–15.

1 Write the words.

coconut ~~sea turtle~~ coral crab jellyfish starfish

1 __sea turtle__   2 _____   3 _____

4 _____   5 _____   6 _____

2 Write true or false.

1 The Great Barrier Reef has a lot of coral islands. _____

2 Coral is a colorful plant. _____

3 The Great Barrier Reef is in Vanuatu. _____

4 You shouldn't touch a box jellyfish. _____

5 Coconut crabs are very small. _____

6 The dodo couldn't fly. _____

3 Complete the sentences.

> animal   bamboo   jellyfish   islands   reefs   towers

1 Coral is an _____ that lives in tropical seawater.

2 Coral skeletons form underwater _____.

3 There are more than 600 coral _____ in the Great Barrier Reef.

4 The box _____ is from the same family as coral.

5 People make houses from _____, and they eat it.

6 In Vanuatu, men dive from tall bamboo _____.

4 Answer the questions.

1 How do waves help to form coral islands?

_____

2 What colors are tropical fish?

_____

3 Why shouldn't you touch a box jellyfish?

_____

4 How does the coconut crab open coconuts?

_____

5 Where did the dodo live?

_____

6 Why didn't the dodo fly?

_____

4 Amazing Island Species

← Read pages 16–19.

1 Complete the words.

1 _jumping_
  spider

2 w_____
  r_____

3 t_____
  k_____

4 G_____
  t_____

5 K_____
  d_____

6 l_____

2 Complete the sentences. Use the words from activity 1.

1 The ____lemur____ has a long tail.

2 There are many _____ on the Galapagos Islands.

3 Scientists discovered a _____ that lives in trees.

4 The _____ _____ can smell things with its tongue.

5 On New Guinea, scientists discovered a giant _____ _____ .

6 They also found a giant jumping _____ .

3 Circle the correct words.

1 Komodo Island is in (Indonesia) / **Ecuador**.

2 The lemur lives on **New Guinea** / **Madagascar**.

3 The Galapagos Islands are in the **Pacific** / **Atlantic** Ocean.

4 Madagascar is in the **Indian** / **Pacific** Ocean.

5 There are jumping spiders on **Komodo Island** / **New Guinea**.

4 Answer the questions.

1 Why doesn't the baobab tree get thirsty?

_____

2 Why do some Galapagos tortoises have a long neck?

_____

3 What eats deer and buffaloes?

_____

4 Why do lemurs have a long tail?

_____

5 Write about some amazing animals that you have seen.

_____

_____

_____

_____

_____

5 Remote Islands

← Read pages 20–23.

1 Find the words. Then complete the chart.

pacificoceansocotraatlanticoceantristandacunha
pacificoceaneasterislandanutaindianocean

Oceans	Islands
Pacific Ocean	A
A	T
I	S
P	E

2 Write *fruit, bird,* or *reptile*.

1 chameleon _____

2 albatross _____

3 lizard _____

4 papaya _____

5 banana _____

6 penguin _____

7 snake _____

8 coconut _____

3 Complete the sentences.

> airport   cold   English   fishermen   telephones   windy

1 The weather on Tristan da Cunha isn't _____ , but it's _____ .

2 Most people are farmers or _____ .

3 They speak _____ .

4 You can't visit by plane because there isn't an _____ .

5 People can communicate with the rest of the world by using the Internet and _____ .

4 Answer the questions.

1 Why are there only eight family names on Tristan da Cunha?

_____

2 What was Easter Island like before people came?

_____

3 What did the Ancient Romans want from the dragon's blood tree? Why?

_____

_____

4 What two things are amazing about a chameleon?

_____

_____

6 Big Islands

← Read pages 24–27.

1 Find the islands. Then write them in order. 1 = biggest, 8 = smallest.

s	u	m	a	b	r	o	n	i	a	n	m
d	k	h	g	r	o	t	f	a	r	g	a
b	a	f	f	i	n	i	s	l	a	n	d
o	n	m	o	t	e	n	u	t	e	d	a
r	h	b	s	a	w	d	m	e	t	h	g
n	a	n	t	i	g	l	a	m	b	o	a
e	e	n	s	n	u	e	t	n	m	n	s
o	j	a	p	a	i	n	r	e	r	s	c
s	g	r	e	e	n	l	a	n	d	h	a
s	o	t	c	o	e	t	r	e	r	u	r
a	d	n	e	t	a	m	t	r	e	s	e

1 *Greenland*

2 _____

3 _____

4 _____

5 _____

6 _____

7 _____

8 _____

2 Write true or false.

1 Only 5,500 people live on Greenland. _____

2 Polar bears hunt in winter. _____

3 Polar bears have black skin. _____

4 There are geysers on New Zealand's South Island. _____

5 Giant wetas live in New Zealand. _____

6 Tasmanian devils live in Asia. _____

3 Complete the sentences.

> are eat fly live smell swim

1 The Inuit people _____ in Greenland.

2 Polar bears can _____ 100 kilometers.

3 Kiwis can't _____ .

4 Giant wetas _____ heavy.

5 Tasmanian devils make a horrible _____ .

6 Tasmanian devils can _____ a lot of meat.

4 Answer the questions.

1 Why do polar bears have big paws?

_____

2 What do the Inuit people and polar bears hunt?

_____

3 Where were the *Lord of the Rings* movies filmed?

_____

4 What is a weta?

_____

5 What does a Tasmanian devil do when it's scared?

_____

6 What is a Tasmanian devil's favorite food?

_____

7 Man-Made Islands

← Read pages 28–31.

1 Complete the puzzle.

1 Inle Lake is in ___ .

2 The Intha people grow ___ on the floating islands.

3 ___ has two airports on man-made islands.

4 Tokyo is in ___ .

5 People built ___ on Odaiba Island.

6 Incheon is in South ___ .

7 The Intha people make floating islands with ___ .

1↓ B
   u   3↓
2→ r
   m
   a
              5↓
4→
6→
7→

2 Match. Then write the sentences.

Odaiba Island is · · · more than 20 kilometers long.
Intha men can row · · · tallest hotels in the world.
Burj Al Arab is one of the · · · about 150 years old.
The Incheon bridge is · · · with their legs.

1 _Odaiba Island is about 150 years old._

2 _____

3 _____

4 _____

3 **Order the words.**

1 build / people / man-made islands. / cities on / Sometimes

<u>Sometimes people build cities on man-made islands.</u>

2 build houses / The Intha people / on stilts.

_____

3 hotels, / stores, / on / Palm Jumeirah. / There are / and homes

_____

4 was / Kansai / man-made island. / the first airport / on a

_____

5 man-made islands. / Five airports / in Japan / are on

_____

4 **Answer the questions.**

1 Why do people build man-made islands?

_____

2 What can you find on Odaiba Island?

_____

3 What do tourists like in Dubai?

_____

4 How tall is the Burj Al Arab hotel?

_____

5 Have you ever been to a man-made island?

_____

8 Protecting Our Islands

← Read pages 32–35.

1 Complete the sentences.

> higher   kill   warmer   ice   life   islands   tourists   dies

1 Earth is getting _____ because there's too much carbon dioxide.

2 More _____ is melting, so the sea level is getting _____ .

3 Some _____ are disappearing.

4 Storms and floods can _____ plants and animals.

5 Coral _____ when seawater gets too warm.

6 When _____ visit small islands, it's sometimes bad for plant and animal _____ .

2 Find and write the words from pages 32–35.

1 four countries

_____ _____ _____ _____

2 two groups of islands

_____ _____

3 three oceans

_____ _____ _____

3 Complete the puzzle.
Then find the secret word.

1 ___ dies in warm seawater.

2 We should ___ our islands.

3 Life on islands is often in ___ .

4 The Global ___ Vault is in Norway.

5 Animal ___ can become extinct.

6 Earth is getting too ___ .

7 Sea ___ are getting higher.

8 Species are protected in a conservation ___ .

9 ___ and floods can kill animals.

10 More ___ is melting.

11 We should use less ___ to make electricity.

12 The ___ on the Maldive Islands is less than 2 meters above sea level.

The secret word is:

4 What islands do you want to visit? Why?

_____

_____

_____

_____

_____

An Islands Map

1 Look at the world map and find these islands. Write the numbers.

☐ Anuta   ☐ Hawaii   ☐ New Guinea

☐ Baffin Island   ☐ Hispaniola   ☐ New Zealand

☐ Borneo   ☐ Honshu   ☐ Socotra

☐ Britain   ☐ Iceland   ☐ Stromboli

☐ Canary Islands   ☐ Jeju   ☐ Sumatra

☐ Easter Island   ☐ Komodo   ☐ Svalbard Islands

☐ Galapagos Islands   ☐ Madagascar   ☐ Tasmania

☐ Great Barrier Reef   ☐ Maldive Islands   ☐ Tristan da Cunha

☐ Greenland   ☐ Mauritius   ☐ Vanuatu

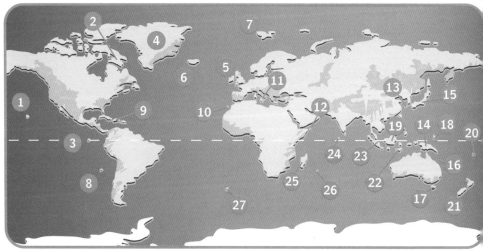

2 Look in books or on the Internet. Find more islands and add them to your map.

Project 2 An Island Poster

1 **Choose an island.**

2 **Look in books or on the Internet and write notes.**

Name of island: _____

Continent: _____

Ocean: _____

Amazing animals: _____

Interesting plants: _____

Weather: _____

Type of island: (Big? Small? Tropical? Volcanic?)

_____

People: (When did people arrive?)

_____

3 **Make a poster. Write about the island and draw a map.
Display your poster.**

Glossary

above on top of

active can erupt (for volcanoes)

adult a person or animal that has finished growing

ankle the part of the body between the foot and the leg

area a part of a place

ash the soft, gray material that you have after a fire

bamboo a tall, tropical plant

become to change into; to start to be

boil to heat a liquid like water until it's so hot it changes into steam

bottom the opposite of top

buffalo (*plural* **buffaloes**) a large animal like a cow

build up to get bigger

canoe a small boat powered with a paddle

carry to take something to another place

change to become different; to make something different

coal old wood that you burn to make fire

communicate to give and receive information

connect to join something with something

conservation area a place where plants and animals are protected

contain to have something inside

continent a very large area of land

cover to put something over something

danger when something could hurt or kill people or animals

dead not living any more

deer (*plural* **deer**) a wild animal

die to stop living

disappear to become impossible to see

disaster something very bad that damages Earth, people, or animals

dive to jump into water or air

drop to let something fall

easily happening in an easy way

electricity a type of energy

enough how much we want or need

erupt to throw out lava (for volcanoes)

escape to get away

evaporate to change from liquid into gas

extinct when a species has died

famous known by many people

far not near

farm a place where farmers grow crops and keep animals

fertile plants can grow well in fertile soil

film to make a movie

fire this is produced when something burns

firewood wood for burning in a fire

float to stay on the top of water

flood where there is a lot of water where it is usually dry

forest a place with a lot of trees

form to make or be made

freeze to change into ice

fresh not old, ready to use

gas (*plural* **gases**) not a solid or liquid; like air or carbon dioxide

giant very large or tall

glacier a large amount of ice, formed by snow in mountains

grass a green plant

ground the land that we stand on

group a number of people or things that are together

grow to get bigger

huge very big

ice frozen water

incredible amazing

insect a very small animal with six legs

jellyfish an ocean animal with long, thin parts like arms

kill to make someone or something die

lake a big area of water

lava hot, liquid rock from a volcano

life all things that live, like animals, plants, and people; how people or things live

mainland land that is part of a continent, not an island

mammal an animal that has babies and feeds its babies milk; people are mammals

man-made made by people; not natural

medicine something that you take when you are sick, to make you better

melt to become liquid because of being hot

middle center

mineral a material, like metal or rock

move to go from one place to another

natural something that comes from nature; not made by people

neck the part of an animal's body that holds up the head

noisy making a loud sound

ocean the salt water that covers most of Earth

oil a black liquid used to make gasoline

poison something that kills or hurts somebody if they eat or drink it

power station a building where electricity is made

problem something that is difficult

produce to grow or make something

protect to keep safe from danger

push to make something move away

remote far from other places

river water on land that goes to the ocean

road vehicles travel on it

rock a very hard, natural material

rocky made from rock

sail a large piece of material that the wind blows on to power a boat; to travel in a ship or a boat using sails or an engine

sandy made from or covered with sand

seahorse a fish that look like a horse

seal an ocean mammal that eats fish

sea level how high the water is in the sea or ocean

seed what a plant grows from

ship a big boat

skeleton all of the bones inside a body

skin a thin layer that covers the outside of an animal or a person

slow down to make something slower

snake an animal with a thin body and no legs

soil the ground that plants grow in

space where the moon and stars are

special different and important

species a group of the same type of animal

spider a very small animal with eight legs

statue the shape of a person or animal often made of stone

steam the hot gas that water makes when it boils

stilts wooden poles

store to keep something to use later

storm very bad weather

surface the outside or the top of something

tail the part of an animal's body that comes out at the back

thick not thin

tiny very small

tongue the part inside the mouth that moves when you speak

tower a tall building

town a place with a lot of buildings, bigger than a village, but smaller than a city

valley the land between hills or mountains

volcanic from a volcano

wave a line of water that moves across the top of the ocean

way how to do something

without not having something; not doing something

wooden made of wood

Oxford Read and Discover

Series Editor: Hazel Geatches • CLIL Adviser: John Clegg

Oxford Read and Discover graded readers are at six levels, for students from age 6 and older. They cover many topics within three subject areas, and support English across the curriculum, or Content and Language Integrated Learning (CLIL).

Available for each reader:
- Audio Pack
- Activity Book

Available for selected readers:
- e-Books

Teaching notes & CLIL guidance: **www.oup.com/elt/teacher/readanddiscover**

Subject Area / Level	The World of Science & Technology	The Natural World	The World of Arts & Social Studies
1 — 300 headwords	• Eyes • Fruit • Trees • Wheels	• At the Beach • In the Sky • Wild Cats • Young Animals	• Art • Schools
2 — 450 headwords	• Electricity • Plastic • Sunny and Rainy • Your Body	• Camouflage • Earth • Farms • In the Mountains	• Cities • Jobs
3 — 600 headwords	• How We Make Products • Sound and Music • Super Structures • Your Five Senses	• Amazing Minibeasts • Animals in the Air • Life in Rainforests • Wonderful Water	• Festivals Around the World • Free Time Around the World
4 — 750 headwords	• All About Plants • How to Stay Healthy • Machines Then and Now • Why We Recycle	• All About Desert Life • All About Ocean Life • Animals at Night • Incredible Earth	• Animals in Art • Wonders of the Past
5 — 900 headwords	• Materials to Products • Medicine Then and Now • Transportation Then and Now • Wild Weather	• All About Islands • Animal Life Cycles • Exploring Our World • Great Migrations	• Homes Around the World • Our World in Art
6 — 1,050 headwords	• Cells and Microbes • Clothes Then and Now • Incredible Energy • Your Amazing Body	• All About Space • Caring for Our Planet • Earth Then and Now • Wonderful Ecosystems	• Food Around the World • Helping Around the World